MARTIAL ARTS IN ACTION

TAE KWON DO

MARTIAL ARTS IN ACTION

TAE KWON DO

BY ANNA HANEY-WITHROW

Marshall Cavendish
Benchmark
New York

This publication represents the opinions and views of the author based on Anna Haney-Withrow's
personal experience, knowledge, and research. The information in this book serves as a general
guide only. The author and publisher have used their best efforts in preparing this book and
disclaim liability rising directly and indirectly from the use and application of this book.

Other Marshall Cavendish Offices:
Marshall Cavendish International (Asia) Private Limited, 1 New Industrial Road, Singapore
536196 • Marshall Cavendish International (Thailand) Co Ltd. 253 Asoke, 12th Flr, Sukhumvit
21 Road, Klongtoey Nua, Wattana, Bangkok 10110, Thailand • Marshall Cavendish (Malaysia)
Sdn Bhd, Times Subang, Lot 46, Subang Hi-Tech Industrial Park, Batu Tiga, 40000 Shah Alam,
Selangor Darul Ehsan, Malaysia

Marshall Cavendish is a trademark of Times Publishing Limited

All websites were available and accurate when this book was sent to press.
Library of Congress Cataloging-in-Publication Data

Haney-Withrow, Anna.
Tae kwon do / Anna Haney-Withrow.
p. cm. — (Martial arts in action)
Includes index.
ISBN 978-0-7614-4940-9 (print)
ISBN 978-1-60870-368-5 (ebook)
1. Tae kwon do—Juvenile literature. I. Title.
GV1114.9.H365 2012
796.815'3—dc22
2010013828

Editor: Peter Mavrikis
Publisher: Michelle Bisson
Art Director: Anahid Hamparian
Series design by Kristen Branch

Photo Research by Candlepants Incorporated

Cover Photo: Mike Powell / Getty Images

The photographs in this book are used by permission and through the courtesy of:
Corbis: © epa, 2; © Leonard de Selva, 14; © Bettmann, 16. *Alamy Images*: © Lucky Look, 6;
© INTERFOTO, 18; © Stock Connection Blue, 20; © Mason Trullinger, 25; © Aflo Foto Agency, 26; ©
Frankalla, 31. *AP Images*: Kevin Sanders, 8; Pat Sullivan, 9. *Getty Images*: LWA, 10, 11; Photo by US Army/
US Army/Time & Life Pictures, 17; Getty Images, 22; Ryan McVay, 23; Mike Powell, 28; Andy Crawford, 29;
Peter Cade, 32; AFP, 33, 35; Julie Toy, 36; Sam Diephuis, 38, 40; Stephen Stickler, 41. *Art Resource, NY*:
The Trustees of the British Museum, 12. *Super Stock*: © Photononstop, 19.

Printed in Malaysia
1 3 5 6 4 2

CONTENTS

CHAPTER ONE

TAEKWONDO STUDENTS AND CHAMPIONS

THE LOPEZ FAMILY of Sugarland, Texas, began their taekwondo (also spelled as tae kwon do) training in earnest in the family garage. During wintertime, their mother would time the laundry so the dryer was running during their training sessions, keeping them warm. Oldest brother Jean was introducing his little brother, Steven, to the art of taekwondo. They worked out relentlessly. Younger siblings Mark and Diana watched their brothers with fascination. It was not long before they too were practicing taekwondo in the family garage. Years earlier, their father Julio, an immigrant from Nicaragua, decided to enroll Jean in what he thought was a karate class to help him develop discipline and good character. In fact, Jean was learning taekwondo. As he developed as an athlete, he

A STUDENT DEMONSTRATES ONE OF THE ATHLETIC KICKS THAT ARE PART OF THE ART OF TAEKWONDO.

THE LOPEZ SIBLINGS, FROM LEFT, STEVEN, DIANA, MARK, AND JEAN LOPEZ AT THE OLYMPIC TAEKWONDO TRIALS.

also developed as a natural coach, serving as a counselor, trainer, and friend to his younger siblings. He pushed them hard to train and reach their fullest potential. And they responded well. Each of the Lopez siblings is a taekwondo champion in his or her own right, competing and winning internationally throughout their youth.

In 2008, this close-knit family accomplished something truly amazing. Siblings Steven, Mark, and Diana all made the United States Olympic Team in taekwondo and competed in Beijing, China. It had been more than one hundred years since the United States had three siblings on an Olympic team. But this accomplishment was even

THE LOPEZ SIBLINGS WORK ON STRETCHING AS PART OF THEIR TAEKWONDO TRAINING.

more remarkable. The coach of the United States Olympic Team was none other than their oldest brother, Jean Lopez. The media quickly nicknamed the Lopezes "the First Family of Taekwondo."

As amazing as the Lopez family story is, it is worth noting that young people all over the world study taekwondo. Competitive fighting, also known as **sparring,** is just one component of this complex martial art. A more typical example of an American taekwondo student might be Jacob. Jacob is ten years old. He attends taekwondo classes two days a week after school, where he learns the various punching, kicking, and blocking techniques.

At his taekwondo school, Jacob has learned to treat his teacher and classmates with a special kind of respect. He studies forms, or *poomsae*, which help him master fighting techniques and develop focus and discipline. Jacob recently was promoted in rank. He took a test and performed the poomsae well. He now wears a different color belt to show his higher rank. Jacob is looking forward to learning to break boards with his striking techniques and someday, as he advances, to begin practicing sparring.

A STUDENT LEARNS FROM HIS SABUMNIM (INSTRUCTOR) DURING A TAEKWONDO PRACTICE.

Jacob is not certain whether competitive sparring, like what the Lopezes do, will be for him or not. He is also involved in the Boy Scouts and likes spending time with his friends. For now, he enjoys taekwondo and the increased confidence it has given him. He likes having something active to do to stay in shape when he is not playing team sports. Jacob has also enjoyed making new friends at his taekwondo school, which includes both boys and girls and students of all ages from many different backgrounds.

A TAEKWONDO STUDENT PRACTICES BREAKING BOARDS.

CHAPTER TWO

HOW KOREA UNITED A MARTIAL ART

TAEKWONDO IS A MARTIAL ART that originated in Korea. The name translates roughly as "the way of foot and hand" or "the way of kicking and punching." Taekwondo is the most widely practiced martial art in the world. Strangely though, taekwondo as we know it has existed just since 1955, when Korea's martial arts masters came together and united under one system. To understand why this extraordinary step was taken, one must understand some history of the Korean peninsula.

What is now considered Korea, long ago, consisted of three distinct kingdoms: Koguryo, Silla, and Paekje. These kingdoms battled one another frequently and also faced conflicts with their neighbors in China and Japan. Each kingdom developed a martial arts style that

MARTIAL ARTS HAVE BEEN PRACTICED IN KOREA FOR THOUSANDS OF YEARS.

IN 1902, THE JAPANESE OCCUPIED SEOUL IN KOREA.

was practiced in society and used to train its soldiers. In the seventh century CE, Silla rulers made an alliance with China and overtook the other kingdoms. The Silla then allied with the Koguryo against the Chinese and essentially united the three kingdoms.

During this time and during the next dynasty, culture and the martial arts flourished. However, in the fourteenth century, the Mongols invaded, and many cultural changes followed. Education and scholarship became more highly prized, and martial arts began to be less widely practiced in the culture. In 1910, Japan took over Korea, and the practice of traditional Korean martial arts was banned.

Koreans, however, continued practicing and teaching their martial arts styles in secret. During this time, many Koreans would have also had the chance to learn more about Japanese and Chinese styles of martial arts, which could have influenced how their styles developed. After World War II, Koreans were free to practice their culture once again, and several martial arts schools, known as *kwans,* opened.

During the 1950s, a civil war erupted in Korea. The military started to train in the traditional Korean martial arts once more, leading to a huge surge in the importance of the kwans. Problems arose, however, because each school emphasized different aspects of philosophy and training. Seeing the need for unification, the masters of the largest schools met on April 11, 1955. They agreed to common rules and practices and united under the name *Tae Soo Do.* Two years later, General Hong Hi Choi, who had been a driving force in training the Korean military to use martial arts, suggested a change of name to taekwondo. It was agreed that name was more

MARINES IN KOREA PRACTICING TRADITIONAL MARTIAL ARTS.

representative of the art, and some noted that it also sounded similar to *Taek Kyon,* one of the arts practiced in the ancient kingdoms.

From this original unified group came two groups who seek to coordinate taekwondo and spread its practice internationally, the International Taekwondo Association and the World Taekwondo Federation. Both groups have organized schools and tournaments worldwide, helping taekwondo to become one of the most widely practiced martial arts around the globe.

A KOREAN SOLDIER DEMONSTRATES HIS MARTIAL ARTS SKILL BY BREAKING BOARDS WITH HIS HEAD.

CHUCK NORRIS

CHUCK NORRIS IS A WORLD-RENOWNED TAEKWONDO MASTER.

One of the most famous practitioners of taekwondo is an American, Chuck Norris. In 1997, Norris became the first American to be awarded an eighth degree black belt in taekwondo. Norris studied taekwondo while stationed in Korea as a member of the United States Air Force. He competed as a karate champion in the 1960s and 1970s. (There were no taekwondo championships at that time.) He retired undefeated in 1974 as the World Professional Middle Weight Karate Champion. He went on to a successful film and television career.

In 1973, the Korean government recognized the World Taekwondo Federation as the governing body for taekwondo as a sport. The first World Championships were held that year. In 1988 and 1992, taekwondo was featured in the Olympics as a demonstration sport. It became a competitive Olympic sport for the first time in 2000 during the Olympic Games in Sydney, Australia.

YOUNG TAEKWONDO STUDENTS IN KOREA PRACTICING POOMSAE.

CHAPTER THREE

STRIKES, KICKS, FORMS, AND COMPETITION

A BEGINNING STUDENT OF TAEKWONDO has much to learn before participating in the type of sparring seen in Olympic competition. Taekwondo is made up of many components, and a student is expected to study each of them. Learning taekwondo involves mastering many techniques, from basic **stances** to high-flying kicks and board breaking. Students also learn the guidelines for behavior and some of the philosophy of taekwondo, like respecting yourself and others.

A taekwondo school is also known as a *dojang.* Each student is expected to wear a white uniform called a *dobok* as well as a belt, the color of which shows his or her ranking or *kup.* The belts for beginners are white. As a student progresses, he or she can improve

A POWERFUL TAEKWONDO KICK CAN KNOCK AN OPPONENT OFF BALANCE.

U.S. SOLDIERS PRACTICING TAEKWONDO.

in kup and move to the next belt color by participating in tests or **gradings.** Even those with black belts continue to learn and improve. Taekwondo offers ten different degrees of black-belt ranking, referred to as *dans.*

A beginning student will first learn the proper way to behave in the dojang, including bowing upon entering or leaving. Students will also bow to the *sabumnim,* the name for taekwondo instructor, at the beginning of each class and to each training partner before and after a training exercise. Bowing is a sign of respect and sincerity. Learning proper etiquette, or expectations for behavior, and

SPARRING PARTNERS BOW TO ONE ANOTHER AS A SIGN OF RESPECT.

developing respect are important factors in mastering the philosophy of taekwondo.

In addition to developing proper etiquette and a sense of respect, students of taekwondo will improve their overall physical fitness. An important part of taekwondo training involves exercises that help students develop flexibility, stamina, and strength. A taekwondo class will typically begin with these exercises to help students improve their abilities and prepare for the rigorous workout ahead.

How to Find a Teacher and Dojang

Pay a visit to a local dojang. Call ahead and express your interest. Ideally, you will be invited to visit a class and meet the sabumnim and some students. Everyone has different needs and expectations, but here are a few things to consider. Does the instructor seem like someone you will be comfortable with? Do the students seem willing to help one another? Is the instructor willing to answer questions you have about insurance, injuries, or other concerns? Is the dojang affiliated with a governing body like the International Taekwondo Federation or the World Taekwondo Federation?

A STUDENT DEMONSTRATES A POWERFUL STRIKE DURING A GRADING.

BASICS

Students first study the basic positions, or **stances**, that form the basis of taekwondo's punching and kicking techniques. Studying stances allows the student to develop the proper balance and footwork necessary to use taekwondo techniques in self-defense or in sparring. Stances involve aligning the feet and arms with the position of the body in a way that allows the martial artist to strike, kick, or **block** most effectively.

THE WAY OF THE HAND: STRIKING TECHNIQUES

Striking techniques involve the hands, arms, and elbows aimed strategically at an opponent. They can be the quickest way a martial artist has to attack an opponent. Common striking techniques include punching, knife hand strikes, and elbow strikes. There are numerous variations of each of these, and there are many details for a student to study about each one. Using these finer points allows a martial artist to deliver strikes that are powerful and well-placed.

A BLACKBELT DEMONSTRATES A POWERFUL PUNCH.

Punching is a common striking technique that looks quite a bit simpler than it really is. A good punch in taekwondo involves making a fist with the thumb bent in front of the first two fingers. Fingers should be tightly closed and the wrist held stiff and kept straight. To maximize the impact of their punches, good martial artists will do several things. First, they will pay attention to the position of their feet. Having good footwork allows fighters to stay stable and defend counterattacks. Also, they will use the positioning of the body to maximize the power of the strike. Finally, they will aim the punch and land it with control. As students advance, they learn the best spots for landing punches.

Open-handed striking techniques, like knife hand strikes, are an important part of studying taekwondo, and students may use them in controlled **one-step sparring** or when learning the taekwondo forms. These techniques are extremely powerful and as such are not suitable to use in sparring. They were developed for serious combat situations, and students must learn to understand and respect the power they have.

THE WAY OF THE FOOT: KICKING TECHNIQUES

Taekwondo places more emphasis on kicking techniques than other martial arts do for several reasons. Because of the length of the leg, kicking is ideal for attacking from a greater distance. Legs are larger and more muscular than arms, so the force of a kick will be greater than that of a strike. Additionally, kicking allows the fighter to incorporate more of the force of the body into each blow.

When learning kicking techniques, students will again want to pay

A STUDENT LANDS A KICK DURING SPARRING.

attention to the stance from which the kick begins. Another important aspect of a kick is the striking surface. Different taekwondo kicks are delivered with different parts of the foot, including the ball, the blade, the sole, the heel, and the front of the foot. Kicking techniques require a lot of practice and concentration because the fighter must deliver the kick correctly and immediately regain his or her balance. Kicking also requires a lot of strength and physical endurance.

ACROBATIC KICKS ARE CONSIDERED A SIGNATURE OF TAEKWONDO.

Once a student has mastered basic kicking techniques, he or she may begin studying how to combine kicking and jumping to deliver flying kicks. These amazing athletic feats are what many think of first when they think of taekwondo. The physical conditioning and balance required to successfully deliver flying kicks come with practice and dedication. Mastering basic kicking techniques is the first step in preparing to study this aspect of the art.

THE ART OF DEFENSE

Part of being an effective taekwondo practitioner is avoiding combat and avoiding an opponent's aggressive moves. A serious martial artist will never fight when it is not necessary. Some conflicts can simply be avoided or walked away from. A sabumnim will give students effective guidelines for making these decisions. When one is fighting in combat or sparring, evading and blocking are the chief defensive techniques available in taekwondo.

Evading is the act of avoiding being struck by an opponent. To become skilled at evading, a student should develop fast, solid footwork and superior mental focus. Evading requires the ability to judge what an opponent is likely to do. It is preferred over blocking because blocking techniques expose a fighter to injury and take greater stamina.

However, evading is often not possible. In this instance, a fighter defends himself or herself using **blocks**. In taekwondo, blocks serve to defend against an opponent's attacks and to weaken the opponent. Blocks can be delivered with either the right or left hand, depending on where the opponent is attempting to strike. Similarly, blocks are

STUDENTS WATCH INTENTLY DURING A TAEKWONDO COMPETITION.

identified as low, middle, or high, depending on what section of the body they are designed to defend.

It may appear that the blocking is done solely with the forearm. However, with practice, the fighter learns to use the power of the legs, hips, and non-blocking arm to strengthen the move. Other more advanced blocks incorporate techniques like reinforcing the block with other parts of the body and using striking techniques within the blocks.

PRACTICE THROUGH POOMSAE

The taekwondo student uses and practices all of the techniques in two ways, through performing poomsae or forms and through

KIHAP!

When observing taekwondo, people often note the loud shouts being made by the practitioners. This practice is known as **kihap**. It is used to incorporate breath control into the art and also to surprise an opponent.

A STUDENT USES KIHAP DURING HER TAEKWONDO PRACTICE.

sparring. Poomsae consist of a series of movements and techniques performed by oneself in a specific sequence. New students will devote time to poomsae before they are ready for sparring. Poomsae remain an important aspect of taekwondo no matter the level of the practitioner. Not only do poomsae help develop fighting skills, but they also help students understand the philosophical principles of taekwondo.

One set of poomsae recognized by the World Taekwondo Federation is called the *Taegeuk.* The Taegeuk consists of eight different poomsae. The poomsae increase in complexity and skill required. Each has a different meaning, and the student's performance of the poomsae should reflect that meaning. In many dojangs, students

A KOREAN MARTIAL ARTIST DEMONSTRATES TAEKWONDO.

practice these forms as a part of the grading procedure that allows them to move from one kup to the next.

When performing poomsae, students should focus on skillful use of the techniques. A good student will also perform the actions with balance and grace, paying attention to body alignment and position. Students should perform poomsae with eyes straight forward as though facing an imaginary opponent. Good performance of poomsae requires advanced mental focus. Students must be fully aware of the present moment and should not be thinking about what has already happened or anticipating the moves ahead.

SPARRING AND SPORT

When a student is ready, he or she will begin sparring in addition to poomsae. Sparring should be supervised by a sabumnim. Students will likely begin with **one-step sparring** in which they are matched with a student of similar rank and size to practice specific techniques. While a student is learning to control his or her movements, one-step sparring is usually no-contact. Students can progress to light-contact sparring as they advance.

Advanced students can participate in full-contact **free sparring,** wearing protective gear including a helmet and pads. Free sparring allows students to test their mastery of techniques as well as their ability to predict and respond to an opponent's moves. Free sparring is a sport practiced with a spirit of respect for opponents. Those who find themselves with feelings of hostility or aggression during sparring are not ready for this aspect of taekwondo training.

In competitive sparring, opponents spar in three minute

rounds (three rounds for men's competition, and two rounds for women's and youth competition). The bout takes place in a 40-by-40-foot (12-by-12-meter) area and is judged by a referee and four judges. The object of a bout is to score more points than one's opponent does. Points are scored by landing blows to a legal target on the opponent or by knocking an opponent down. A kick to the head earns two points. Fighters must follow rules that ensure their safety and the safety of the opponent. Many striking and kicking techniques are prohibited in sparring. Using a prohibited technique or

OLYMPIANS COMPETE IN A TAEKWONDO SPARRING MATCH.

breaking other safety rules will result in a deduction of points, a warning, or possibly disqualification from competition.

The ideas of competing and winning championships are appealing to many young people. But the benefits of practicing taekwondo go far beyond the competitive arena. The study and dedication required for all aspects of taekwondo will serve the practitioner in many facets of life.

THE STUDY OF TAEKWONDO can have amazing benefits, beginning with the obvious physical benefits of being in good shape. Practicing the demanding taekwondo techniques, whether in poomsae or in sparring, leads to the development of cardiovascular fitness, the ability of the heart and lungs to function at their best. Also, taekwondo practice will result in building lean muscle, making the practitioner stronger and healthier overall.

Students of taekwondo often report dramatic increases in self-esteem and self-confidence. These feelings may be due, in part, to the healthy conditioning of the body. But studying taekwondo also helps students understand how to deal with conflict appropriately, how to treat others with respect, and how to act with courage and self-

*STUDENTS OF TAEKWONDO ARE PHYSICALLY FIT AND FEEL GOOD
ABOUT THEMSELVES.*

control. These character attributes surely promote self-confidence as well.

The driving principle behind taekwondo is peace. Students develop a sense of inner peace by learning how the mind and body work together and by developing the focus necessary to practice taekwondo effectively. The philosophy involved in taekwondo is derived from many ancient Eastern traditions and is reflected in taekwondo training. Taekwondo practitioners believe that by

STUDENTS OF TAEKWONDO DEVELOP A SENSE OF PEACE BY LEARNING HOW THE BODY AND MIND WORK TOGETHER.

Autism and Martial Arts

Taekwondo seems particularly helpful for individuals on the autism spectrum, who may have challenges with coordination and balance. Parents also report an increase in students' abilities to follow directions and get along with others. Like many students, children on the autism spectrum may see an increase in self-confidence from their taekwondo study.

TAEKWONDO CAN HELP MANY STUDENTS INCREASE THEIR FITNESS AND THEIR SELF-ESTEEM.

Taegeuk
Poomsae

Each of the Taegeuk poomsae has a meaning that students come to understand through practice and guidance from their teachers.

Il Jang – Heaven and creation

Yi Jang – Firm on the inside and soft on the outside

Sam Jang – Brightness and heat

Sah Jang – Thunder: great power and dignity

Oh Jang – Wind: both forceful and calm

Yuk Jang – Water: always flowing and soft

Chil Jang – Mountain: firmness and stability

Pal Jang – Earth: receptiveness, the beginning and the end

EAGER STUDENTS HEAD INTO A TAEKWONDO PRACTICE.

practicing the physical aspects of taekwondo and by living with respect and a desire for unity with others, students will come to understand taekwondo philosophy.

For serious students, taekwondo becomes a way of life that helps them develop their potential and helps them to serve others. The World Taekwondo Federation advises, "To ultimately enable ourselves to lead more valuable lives, we would do well by finding the guiding principles deeply hidden in taekwondo."

GLOSSARY

block—A move, often done with a forearm, used to neutralize an opponent's attack.

dan—Degree or level of black belt ranking.

dobok—A taekwondo uniform.

dojang—A taekwondo school or training hall.

evading—Avoiding an opponent's attack by ducking or moving to the side.

free sparring—Taekwondo practice in which opponents try to anticipate one another's moves and land blows.

grading—A test taken to move from one ranking to the next.

kihap—Loud yell used to control the breath and startle the opponent.

kup—A level of ranking below the black belt level.

kwan—Korean martial arts school.

one-step sparring—Taekwondo practice in which students try specific techniques in pairs, with one as the aggressor and one as the defender.

poomsae—Forms or specific sequences of moves practiced to master taekwondo techniques and philosophy.

sabumnim—A taekwondo instructor.

sparring—Taekwondo practice in which two participants act as opponents.

stance—A standing position from which a strike or kick begins.

Tae Soo Do—The original name given to taekwondo upon the unification of Korea's martial arts schools.

Taegeuk—A set of eight poomsae learned by many students of taekwondo.

Taek Kyon—A martial arts style practiced in ancient Korea.

FIND OUT MORE

BOOKS

Gifford, Clive. *Taekwondo* (Sporting Skills). London: Wayland Publishing, 2010.

Macaulay, Kelly and Bobbie Kalman. *Taekwondo in Action* (Sports in Action). New York: Crabtree Publishing, 2004.

Pawlett, Mark, and Ray Pawlett. *The Tae Kwon Do Handbook*. New York: Rosen Publishing, 2004.

WEBSITES

Taekwondo—Olympic.org
http://www.olympic.org/en/content/Sports/All-Sports/Taekwondo/

TIME for Kids – Around the World – South Korea
http://www.timeforkids.com/TFK/kids/hh/goplaces/
main/0,28375,927166,00.html

World Taekwondo Federation
http://www.wtf.org

INDEX

Page numbers in **boldface** are illustrations.

ABOUT THE AUTHOR

Anna Haney-Withrow is a writing teacher at Florida Gulf Coast University in Fort Myers, Florida. She has practiced a Chinese martial art known as tai chi.